Conflict Resolution Handbook:

Managing Violence and Aggression in the Workplace

By

Daniel Jones

GHR (Reg.), GQHP, DHypPsych(UK), D.NLP, HypPrac

BSYA (B.D, Cur.Hyp, H.Md, Zen.Md) MASC (Relax, NLP)

Conflict Resolution Instructor

Contact the author:

www.personalfreedom.co.uk

First Printed Edition 2007

Copyright © Daniel Jones 2005

Daniel Jones asserts the moral right to be identified as the author of this work

All rights reserved. No part of this publication may be reproduced, stored in a retrieval system, or transmitted, in any form or by any means, electronic, mechanical, photocopying, recording, or otherwise, without the prior written permission of the publishers or author.

ISBN 978-1-4092-2287-3

1 First Edition 1

Acknowledgements

Thank you to Abbie Piper for her on going support and love. Thank you to Kim Piper (no relation to the previous Piper), Jackie Hooper, Dave Holland, and the rest of you (you know who you are), that have worked in challenging situations with me and more.

Thank you also to the late Pat Beyer for always being so kind and supportive, and John Robbins for the training he gave me.

Thank you also to everyone that I have worked with over the years in difficult situations, your support has always been appreciated.

And finally thank you to Graham Levell and to Dr David Lewis & Darren Bridger for their encouragement, support and ideas.

Contents

Introduction	9
The mistakes made by many other conflict resolution books and courses	15
Key terms	31
Territories and personal space, cultural differences & reducing the risks of violence	35
An Understanding of Anger and how it controls the mind of the aggressor	57
The difference between aggression aimed at you and at others, and how to manage incidents	63
The importance of having an awareness of the aggressors basic emotional needs	77
What is necessary to remember when confronted with aggression or violence	87
Non-physical strategies for managing aggression or its onset	97
Bullying	117
Finally	121
Bibliography	123
Index	127

Introduction

Under the Health and Safety at Work Act 1974 and changes to Reporting of Injuries, Diseases and Dangerous Occurrences Regulations 1995 (RIDDOR) employers have a duty of care for reducing the risk of harm from violence, ensuring that staff receive adequate training and guidance.

Any harm caused by violence has to be reported just like any other accident or injury caused whilst the employee is carrying out their duty.

Any death caused by failure of an employer to ensure that the risk of injury from violence is reduced can result in the employer being found negligent and can lead to a manslaughter prosecution.

Not all employers can afford the thousands of pounds that it can cost to send staff on training courses to learn how to manage violent and aggressive situations.

Even when employers do send staff on these courses the staff will still need regular refresher courses which means further expense on the part of the employer every six months or so.

Added to this is the cost of training all new staff when they start employment. In the nursing and care sectors especially where there is an increased risk of encountering violence or aggression and a high staff turnover, it can be impractical to not have staff on shift. Or have under skilled staff on shift, until you have enough staff to make the cost of training them worthwhile.

What is taught in this book is based on the latest understandings of anger and what it needs to keep it burning. From these understandings come a number of skills and abilities that you can learn that avoid supplying that fuel the anger so desperately requires.

Most of the skills and techniques are based on refining natural responses. By doing this it makes them easier to learn and remember and turn into instinctive responses.

This book contains a variety of effective de-escalation techniques and explains how to manage the aftermath of an incident and how to support anyone distressed by an aggressive incident.

The book is designed in a way that allows it to be incorporated into your current training courses, or to be used to update and compliment existing courses on restraint training or managing aggression.

This book has been written to teach how to manage violence and aggression that is directed at you and others within the workplace.

In my working career within the care and the retail industries I have been involved in over 1000 incidents involving high levels of violence and aggression, with over 300 of these potentially being life threatening.

This book is based on skills and experiences that I have gained over the years to create an effective approach to managing violence and aggression whilst maintaining your own safety and the safety of others around you.

All of the skills and techniques that you will be reading about and learning have been tried and tested successfully on many occasions in real life situations.

In many professions, like the care sector, or nursing, or teaching, the staff often have to maintain their duty of care for the person being aggressive. If the staff cause pain to the aggressor they are likely to also cause long term harm to their relationship with that person.

At the end of most of the chapters there are some exercises that you can do if you are using this for training purposes

It is advisable that you incorporate into regular staff meetings a section on dealing with violence and aggression in your workplace. Preferably also having an experienced and highly competent person to offer to demonstrate any techniques if necessary. In this section of the staff meeting, any issues relating to aggressive incidents that have happened or any ongoing aggressive incidents can be discussed and strategies for managing them or refreshers of techniques can take place.

I also recommend that you have a daylong refresher every six months or so to keep the contents of this book freshly in mind where all the staff can also take time to discuss issues relating to the management of violence and aggression. Unfortunately many companies don't discuss the topic of how to manage violence and aggression if it should arise. They just ignore the subject until it happens. By then it is too late. I have known staff to find themselves in highly challenging situations with no guidance on what to do, how to manage the situation, who to contact, what recording and reporting is required. All of these issues should be raised in the same way as every employee should know fire procedures.

The mistakes made by many other conflict resolution books and courses

There are a number of courses and training products available that teach about staff safety in violent or aggressive situations. These courses teach a number of techniques that on the surface can sound sensible and logical. Unfortunately they are all techniques that often don't work very well, or at worst can cause even greater aggression or violence.

This isn't necessarily the fault of the trainers. Often the course content has been adapted from elsewhere. It could be that a psychologist came up with the course by just thinking about how to communicate effectively, or the course was created many years ago and was flawed and had never been up dated as developments in human understanding and in neurology and psychology have been made.

In my experience there seems to generally be two types of conflict resolution training. The type that is formed by psychologists or others that have never really been in regular situations involving high levels of aggression or violence.

These courses will have a few basic verbal strategies and a few basic body language techniques. They may describe what to look out for in a person that lets you know they are angry or likely to get angry. They will often explain mental processes and be full of psychological jargon. They might not be too full of physical techniques for maintaining safety.

The other type of conflict resolution is the type formed by people that have been in conflicts. They may have received self-defence or martial arts training in the past.

These courses generally will have a high level of physical strategies, often all pain compliant techniques involving joint locks and pressure points. They will usually have very little training in psychological skills or understandings.

The problem with nearly every course that I have been aware of to date is that they are too focused on one area of the issue, either psychology or physical techniques. They rarely teach non-pain compliant techniques and they rarely teach about conflict resolution in line with all the latest information from psychology, neurology and human behaviour. Often they overlook the basic human needs of the aggressor and how the aggressor can be helped, even if it is just very minimally.

Over the next few chapters I will cover some of the areas that other courses cover as strategies for managing violence and aggression.

Rapport

Most people have heard about rapport. Rapport is like a dance. People in rapport act similar to each other. You can see it when you walk into a bar. You can look around the bar and see which people are behaving the most similar. They will be the people that are in good rapport with each other.

Rapport is the quality of a relationship that comes from mutual trust and responsiveness. You gain rapport by understanding and respecting the way another person sees the world. Rapport is essential for good communication. If you have rapport others will feel acknowledged and immediately be more responsive.

The difficulty with the use of rapport when dealing with somebody that is violent or aggressive is that to build rapport you need to act similar to the other person.

As the aggressive person isn't likely to calm down and be similar to you, you would have to be similar to them. This means that you would have to get aggressive or at least act aggressive. Clearly in this context if you were to raise your voice and to begin to act aggressively then it would make the aggressor get more defensive about their point of view and be more aggressive back.

I have seen this in many incidents. People think that they need to build rapport to deal with someone that is aggressive. They start to give similar body language, begin to raise their voice, they stand up. The trouble with all of this is that then they are giving off signals that we normally receive when we are being threatened. So no longer is it a situation with one aggressor and one victim, it is now two aggressors aiming their aggression at each other.

As I will cover later, when someone becomes aggressive, because they are highly emotional they respond with black or white thinking. This thinking is the 'I'm right, you're wrong' type of thinking. At the same time they go into 'fight or flight' mode. They are being aggressive so they have already decided that fighting is the option, in this mode of thinking they will pick up on any signal of threat as something to fight (to eliminate that threat)

If you are building rapport with the aggressor you become that threat.

There are times when building rapport can work very well in conflict resolution. For example: building rapport can work very well when dealing with someone that is considerably calmer. Correct use of rapport can help to prevent a potential aggressor from becoming aggressive. It doesn't work when the person is already angry.

If you use rapport when you first notice someone is beginning to become agitated then you are in a position where you can calm them down and avoid a situation from occurring.

You can also use rapport to blend in with a group (as long as you don't come across as fake and copying) to avoid a situation from arising or to avoid becoming a target because you will be acting like 'one of them'.

Acting non-threatening

Another regularly taught skill for managing aggression is to act non-threatening. By this I mean to set up your body language in a way that is supposed to portray calmness and passiveness to avoid aggravating the situation.

This again sounds like good advice. The difficulty with this option is that when someone is on the receiving end of violence or aggression they rarely genuinely feel calm and relaxed.

What happens is that if they try to fake being calm and they try to make themselves look non-threatening they are going against all of the unconscious signals that they are giving off.

The angry person in their highly emotional state is predominantly going to respond to body language more than the words used, so even though they are trying to look calm it will in fact make them look more nervous or perhaps like they are hiding something.

For example:

If you put your hands behind your back and you stand square on to the aggressor trying to look relaxed, you have firstly offered them a large target to aim for if they become violent.

Secondly with your hands behind your back the aggressor could feel that you are hiding something.

Also if you decide to cross your arms to try to appear calm or to hide the nervousness or shaking they may take this as not paying them the attention they are trying to get. It can give off a signal suggesting that you don't care, which again can cause them to become more aggressive.

Telling the aggressor to calm down

Often courses teach that you should try to calm the aggressor down. Most people take this to mean talking about calming down. In my experience it is OK to occasionally mention calming down, usually in conjunction with other ideas. For example:

Saying 'we could go and sit down over there and calm down a little and talk about this. Then I can see how I can help'.

Or

'If you calm down a little I can keep up with what you are saying then I can see how I can help you'

If you just keep talking about calming down regardless of what the aggressor is saying then they often feel that you are not listening at all and so they become increasingly angry. Everyone has either seen or experienced having someone telling a person that is angry to calm down and the angry person gets angrier saying 'I don't want to fucking calm down'

It rarely works. It usually just aggravates the aggressor further which in turn is going to make the situation harder to manage.

As far as possible in situations that I have been involved in I do my best to avoid telling someone to calm down. I may imply it by taking a pronounced sigh or by sitting down. But I know that if I actually say it to the aggressor they are likely to take it as me trying to tell them what to do and trying to tell them to do something they don't want to do right then.

Most people have experienced getting annoyed about something and wanting to complain. They phone a complaints department or a customer services department and all they want is to be able to vent their well rehearsed (in their mind) complaint at the person on the other end. They don't want to calm down, they want to say what their complaint is and why they are right and what they think should be done about it.

This is a common situation to everyone. The aggressor also will have probably gone over in their mind why they need to complain or behave in a certain way. They need to vent it all before you can mention calming down, or any other ideas. They need to focus on what they feel they need to say.

Your customers/clients/patients come first

Another idea that is taught to staff is that customers or patients or clients come first.

This idea if stuck to can cause staff to remain in situations that are dangerous, and that are beyond their control.

This idea is a dangerous one because if the situation is out of control, how exactly do you put the customer first?

What do you plan on doing? If you are there because you feel duty bound even though the situation is out of your control, you are likely to get hurt as well as your customer's.

The best option would be to get help or to call the police unless you know of another strategy for the situation that might work that doesn't put anyone at further risk. This way you are doing what you can to protect your customers whilst at the same time not putting yourself at risk.

It is always very commendable to see staff putting customer's first, but you have to think about the risks. It may be that you feel relatively safe in the situation and that by showing presence even though you can't technically do anything to alter the situation or make it better, the customer's feel better. This is different to putting your customer's first in the sense that I'm thinking of.

What I'm talking about is where you put yourself at risk so that you and the customer's are likely to get hurt now. It can be controversial to suggest not putting your customer's first as it is something that is taught on so many courses. What I'm saying is that you should do your utmost best for your customer's without seriously compromising your safety. You are doing your best for your customer's if you call the police to report that your shop has a gang armed with knives ransacking the store, and then you wait where you are safely.

If you do nothing you would be being negligent so you would have to do something. If you went into the shop front (believing you were putting yourself at a high level of risk) just to try to protect the customer's even though you know you can't do anything then you are likely to get seriously injured which wouldn't have been sensible.

Be assertive

The final idea that many courses teach you to do is to be assertive.

They will teach you how to say what you want in a way that respects the other person's feelings, in a way that is supposed to be non-aggressive.

They will have you saying 'I feel' or 'I think' to start sentences rather than 'You make me feel'. The difficulty with this is that although it is useful when you need to sound sure and confident and unwavering for returning goods to shops or for refusing to do overtime, it comes across as threatening and aggressive when used with someone that has a high level of anger.

This is because, as I will cover shortly, the angry person is thinking from a different part of the brain and in a different way to how a calmer person would be thinking.

It is a useful technique or skill to use to defuse situations before the emotional intensity rises too high because it does focus solely on how you feel and what you think without putting any blame onto the other person.

Unfortunately if it is used with someone that is already in a highly aggressive state of mind they are likely to feel that what you are saying and they way you are saying it is a direct threat because in their state of mind that is how it sounds.

Everybody has had the experience of this sort of thing. For example, when someone is depressed or upset and you say something that under normal circumstances you know they would find funny but the issue is perhaps too emotional for them so they take offence or get more upset.

I remember when I was a senior member of staff in retail catering, when staff would be rushed off their feet to lighten the mood I would often joke with them and comment on them not doing enough work. The staff knew I was just joking and would just smile and joke back. One day a member of staff (unknown to me) had had a really rough few days, they had kept it bottled up and tried to carry on working like normal. When they were really busy and I tried to joke with them they took what I said personally as if I had said it as an attack on them. I had said virtually the same thing to them many times before and to dozens of other people, but this once they were in a state of mind where they got angry over what I said.

They went away, had a break and calmed down, and then we talked about it and worked things out. I learnt why they got angry so quickly, and why they took what I said personally. At the end of the day there were no hard feelings, we were getting on fine like normal. The reaction was all down to the state of mind of the person at the time I gave my comment.

Although this scenario doesn't involve assertiveness it demonstrates the same principle that people can take things the wrong way if they are in the wrong state of mind. So being assertive to someone that is aggressive can be interpreted by them as you being aggressive towards them.

Key terms

There are a number of terms that are useful to know and to understand.

The first term is Reasonable Force

What is reasonable force?

Reasonable force is where:

- You use the minimum amount of force necessary to prevent the potential harm that could occur in the situation
- The more serious the danger the greater degree of force you can use
- What constitutes reasonable comes down to a matter of judgement

This judgement will be based on training, experience and your knowledge of the situation and people involved

The next term is Negligence

Negligence is where you have:

- Breached your duty of care
- Or where you have failed to carry out your duty of care
- Or where any damage or harm is sustained to anybody due to failure to carry out part of your duty of care or
- Where you took no action

For example if you mopped the floor and knew that you were supposed to put down a wet floor sign but didn't and somebody slipped you would be negligent. Or if you saw two children in your care fighting and you thought it will be fine they'll stop in a minute and then one of them got seriously injured when you could have intervened, you would be negligent.

If you don't feel that you could enter a situation and help so you take no action you would be negligent so you must take action, even if it is getting help, or calling the police.

Next is Assault

An assault is:

- An attempt by force or by violence to do bodily injury to another
- It is an act of aggression done against or upon another person without their consent
- And it is not necessary for actual physical harm to take place. If for example, an object was thrown but missed, and there was the ability of the aggressor to use violence then this will constitute an assault
- An assault may also be legally defined on the apprehension that an immediate battery is to be inflicted or done

The last definition is battery:

- Which is intentionally bringing about harmful or offensive contact with a person without their consent

Territories and personal space, cultural differences & reducing the risks of violence

Now to move on from what other courses teach that are often counter-productive to learning what can help you to manage violence and aggression more effectively.

Everyone has a personal space that when violated can cause you to feel uncomfortable. Studies done by the Police on crowd control found that the aggression level of the whole crowd grew as the crowd became more dense and that the aggression level reduced when people were more spread out.

Generally you have 4 areas of personal space. Intimate, personal, social and public. Usually intimate space is distances up to 50cm from your body, personal is distances up to about 1.2m, social is up to 3.6m and public space is distances greater than 3.6m.

If someone intrudes into your Intimate space it causes physiological changes to occur within your body like your heart pumping faster, and increased adrenaline in your blood all preparing you for 'fight or flight'.

This is because it is very close to you and so can be very intimidating if permission wasn't given for the person to get that close. This doesn't mean that permission has to be given verbally to the other person. It can just be that you don't mind or would quite like them to get that close.

When people are in your personal space, which is within a distance of 1.2 metres, if they are someone that you know then you can feel comfortable with this. If they are someone that you don't know then you may begin to feel a little uncomfortable or a little uneasy.

Different cultures have different distances for their spaces. For example some cultures involve touching while communicating more than other cultures. If you are someone who feels uncomfortable being touched by a stranger or by someone that you don't really know then this behaviour can begin to reduce your tolerance to getting angry. Generally the more sparsely populated the place is that someone is from or that someone lives the more personal space they want.

If your job involves people being in crowded situations, like in a crowded waiting room or in a crowded shop or queue certain things are more likely to happen

1. People feel they are not permitted to speak to anyone
2. They avoid eye contact at all times
3. They maintain an emotionless poker face
4. If they have a book or newspaper they may appear deeply engrossed in it
5. The bigger the crowd the less movement they feel they can make which can lead to a reduced tolerance to anger
6. In lifts and waiting rooms they normally feel compelled to look at the floor numbers or something else to keep their attention and stop them making eye contact with anyone

It can be useful, if your workplace is crowded, to think about what changes can be made to reduce the crowding. Could the layout be changed? Could the way customer's or patients get dealt with be altered to allow more freedom?

Anyone that has been stuck in a crowd (or a traffic jam) knows what it can feel like. It is important, as a staff team to focus on changes that will create an environment that is more customer/patient friendly. An environment that helps calmness rather than promoting aggression and stress.

The same is also true in nightclubs and bars. If the environment is too crowded then there is likely to be a rise in violence and aggression. It is important to monitor the numbers of customer's in the venue and to keep them at a level that isn't overcrowded.

It can be nice to have a packed out bar or club and to know the venue is making plenty of money, but is it worth the cost to staff and customer safety from violence and aggression.

Reducing the risk of aggression

On many courses de-escalation is often taught as something that you do when a situation has already escalated. The difficulty with only de-escalating the situation when it has escalated is that by then the aggressor has entered a focused state of aggression and won't be able to be reasoned with.

What should be done instead is to think about de-escalation right from the start. Think about de-escalation and prevention measures that reduce the level of aggression just as the aggression is starting.

There are a number of useful techniques and skills that you can learn to reduce the risk of aggression and to de-escalate situations.

Thinking before you speak, not winding people up

So often people say what they think without thinking about how that communication is going to be received. It could be an unhelpful comment or it could be a comment that appears argumentative.

By thinking before speaking the communication you give is likely to more productive. There are a number of other advantages to thinking before speaking. When you do this you slow down your responses, this makes you look calmer. You also appear to be listening to what the aggressor has to say because you will give more periods of silence.

Keeping people informed or involved

When you keep people involved and informed it makes people feel respected and valued. It also takes away a key piece of potential fuel for any aggression. They can't argue that you didn't keep them informed. They may still be annoyed at waiting but they are more likely to not resort to violence or aggression.

For example;

If someone is waiting for their appointment in a hospital and they had been given an appointment time and they had already been waiting an hour passed that appointment time. If no-one has informed them why there is a long wait they are likely to feel that they have been forgotten, and they are likely to begin to get angry.

If on the other hand they turn up and are told almost straight away that there is currently a delay of up to an hour but that the Doctor is sorry. The patient may still be annoyed but is less likely to act on that irritation at the situation because they know they have a time they have been told that they should be seen. It could even be the case that they are told that due to the long wait they could go off if they wanted and return in forty-five minutes time.

All of this would help to prevent a situation from occurring because you would be thinking about the patient and their needs and how best you can make their situation as comfortable as possible.

People like to feel that they are being involved and consulted, not ignored.

Offering good choices

In many situations staff make the mistake of only offering negative options.

For example;

If you work in a shop and you suspect someone of planning on shoplifting you have two options. You can either stop them now before they steal anything or you can wait until they leave the shop and catch them with stolen goods.

Unfortunately most staff seem to want to catch the shoplifters rather than prevent them. The trouble with catching them is that they then have nothing to lose. The shop staff may stop them at the exit and say they need to come back into the office because they have been caught stealing.

The shoplifter knows that if they go with the staff they will get arrested so they will want to fight for freedom. Often the situation will be made worse by the staff telling them 'are you going to come in on your own or do we have to drag you in' this obviously leaves no room for a positive outcome.

If on the other hand the shop staff approach the potential shoplifter when they first suspect them and offer them a basket to carry their goods in the shoplifter knows they have been seen but haven't been accused of anything. They have the chance to put the goods back or to pay for them and leave with no trouble.

To offer good choices you need to make sure that there are options that offer an escape for the aggressor (or potential aggressor). If all of the options lead to negative outcomes then you are likely to encounter trouble.

In childcare I have known of many staff that would tell the children, if they didn't go to bed they would have their television removed from their room for a week. When the child didn't go to their room and they had their television removed they would play up every night for the whole week because they have nothing to lose.

When on the other hand the staff removed the television but said they could have it back when they have gone to bed on time three nights in a row, then the child would improve their behaviour because that is what gets them their television back. The control is in their hands no the hands of the staff. If they mess around night after night then they are choosing not to have their television back, it's not the staff making that decision.

The mistake of thinking 'it won't happen to me'

So often especially in care work staff believe that they know the client and don't believe that they will be at risk. If there is evidence to say that someone has a history of violence then necessary precautions to reduce risk should be taken.

It is foolish to over look potential risks based on unfounded beliefs. I knew someone that thought 'it won't happen to me' when they took a teenager out for a walk along a beach alone. They refused to have someone go with them. They were sure that as this teenager had always been good with them so far since being in the care home they felt the teenager wouldn't be a problem.

They completely ignored the years of history of this young person. When they got to the beach and were alone, the young person stole the car keys and then physically assaulted the member of staff. She had been so sure this wouldn't happen because in the few months he had been in the home there hadn't been any similar problems.

It isn't the case that you don't offer people increasing levels of trust. What you do is you carryout risk assessments and have action plans in place detailing what you would do if the worst should happen.

It could be that you have a set time to call in and if you don't call by that time people will carryout the action plan. Or perhaps you have someone that will walk past the room you are in and glance through the window every few minutes, or you will use a room where the door can stay ajar.

If you always plan for the worst and expect the best, then if anything happens you will have done all the preparation that you could do. If nothing happens then it doesn't matter because the preparation in risk assessments will be checked regularly and adapted but will not need to be re-written in each situation so staff will always know what to do. Never think 'it will never happen to me', this just makes you more vulnerable.

Trust your intuition

In modern day society people seem to ignore their intuition. They will feel that something isn't right but think that they are just being stupid to think like that.

For example;

A social worker arriving at a patient's house may feel uncomfortable with the way that the patient is behaving. Perhaps it is something minor that causes this feeling like the patient perhaps drawing the curtains or maybe the patient suggests sitting in a different room to normal. It may even (as is often the case) be that the social worker feels uncomfortable but doesn't know why. Unfortunately despite feeling uncomfortable the social worker may enter the situation and then get attacked.

Quite often attacks occur when staff members enter into situations that they claim later made them feel uncomfortable but they ignored it and didn't act on it.

If you feel uncomfortable think of a way of avoiding being in the situation, or think of a way of having another member of staff in that situation with you. Or perhaps you could suggest that you and the patient sit in a café to talk instead of in their home. Or rather than going into a young persons room in a care home if you feel that they may attack you, perhaps you could either get another member of staff to be around near to the young person's room. If all the staff are busy downstairs with other young people then you may ask the young person to come downstairs to the lounge to talk a minute.

There are always ways that you can maintain your safety and prevent situations from arising. Never let yourself feel pressured into compromising your safety. It is important to trust your instincts even if you don't know why you feel a certain way. Obviously your instinct may be wrong and they may have been no threat. You don't know this though. It is better to be safe than sorry.

Don't be afraid to lose face

Often staff don't want to lose face in front of others. It could be a train conductor that has a passenger that refuses to show his ticket. The conductor might not want to lose face in front of all of the passengers that are looking on and so might get more forceful in his approach to avoid losing face.

Or a manager stopping a shoplifter may threaten to drag the shoplifter back to the office if he doesn't come quietly because he doesn't want to lose face in front of the other staff.

If you don't mind risking losing face you are likely to make better decisions.

If the conductor on a train can accept losing face, then he can think of alternatives. He can suggest the passenger shows his ticket or gets off at the next stop. He could just carry on checking tickets and not make a scene, just perhaps simply stating that a ticket needs to be shown to be able to travel on the train and asking if they are deciding not to show a ticket, then when further down the train calling for transport police to deal with it at the next stop.

The manager of the shop could offer the shoplifter a basket to carry goods in that look like they are about to steal. This would prevent the shoplifter from actually committing a crime.

It could be that you could say that the potential aggressor is right about a point of view even if by agreeing you think you will lose face. People always say pride comes before a fall. If you want to always look good in front of people then you are likely to have that fall. You are likely to be involved in more serious situations. If you can be prepared to lose face then you are likely to be capable of more flexible behaviour and decisions. This means you will be likely to have less serious incidents.

Take calculated risks and don't worry about being embarrassed

If you are prepared to take small risks you may be able to do things to stop situations from happening. I don't mean taking risks in aggressive situations but taking risks to prevent situations from occurring.

For example, taking a risk to approach a potential shoplifter even if you find it embarrassing to offer them a basket to carry the items they have.

So many people find situations embarrassing and think they couldn't approach someone to ask if they need a basket or if they need any help, or asking someone if they want to talk. By overcoming this fear of what they might say or how they might respond, people can increase their chances of having far fewer incidents arising.

Get out of situations that you can't manage, get help

If possible do this in a non-obvious way.

If you notice a situation is getting out of control you can say something like 'I'll just check with someone and be back in a minute'. Saying something like this will often work well giving you a chance to get help or to give them time to calm down while at the same time it will give you time to think about how to manage the situation.

You could keep going away and coming back telling them you are just doing something like checking with the manager. As long as you always keep them informed of what is going on often they will be willing to wait which gives them time to calm down.

Whenever you do anything that calms someone down they are less likely to respond with anger or have the incident flare up again. It also allows you a chance to keep calm and to appear to always be helping the potential aggressor.

Let them vent their anger verbally, make responses that show you are listening

When someone is angry they have things that they want to say. Often they will have spent lots of time planning exactly what they were going to say and how the incident was going to pan out before they came face to face with you.

What you should do is make sounds and responses to show you are listening, like making an 'mmm' sound or nodding your head, or occasionally feeding back some of what they say to you.

Usually the whole time that someone is verbally venting their anger they are not so likely to get physically aggressive because they are focusing on saying what they have got to say.

When the aggressor feels listened to they will begin to calm down because they have no need to be defensive. If someone has nothing to fight against because they are being agreed with and apparently helped then they have nothing to attack. Sometimes it could be that you come across as being on the same side as the aggressor and you are both attacking what it is they see as the issue.

You can give appropriate commands to calm the person down

Because angry people are in a trance state they respond to simple non-threatening commands.

If you say something like 'take a seat (a direct command) and I'll be back in a minute' they are likely to sit down which immediately starts calming them down whilst walking away for a few minutes will then give them a little more time to calm down.

Only from practising can most people get proficient at giving commands in this manner.

As above, to make the commands more powerful and more likely to work you can link them with another behaviour, preferably a behaviour that is inevitable. This makes the command more likely to work for two reasons. Firstly, if there is a statement that is true and inevitable that the command is linked to, then this inevitable behaviour happening causes the command to take effect. Secondly, if you link the command with a statement about another behaviour then the person will focus on the other behaviour and ignore the suggested command, this makes it more likely to happen because the command sneaks past the aggressors mental defences and is let in to their mind.

Apologise, even if you don't believe it is your fault

If you apologise it removes fuel from the aggression. It doesn't matter if you aren't to blame, what you want is to calm the situation down.

Keep distance

When someone is angry they respond instinctively.

If they see sudden movements they are likely to strike out in response. It is important that you have some distance so that hand gestures and other movements can be clearly seen. Also for an aggressor to hit you when you are further away takes a little more thought which involves the conscious part of the brain and so can be enough to stop them carrying it out.

For example;

If a wife slapped her husband during an argument and she was stood near to him, he may hit her back without any thought and then regret it afterwards and wonder what possessed him.

Watch your body language

About 95% of the information that we perceive from others is the body language that they use. We often don't consciously think about this, we just respond to it unconsciously.

It is important to keep your body language non-threatening.

By having non-threatening body language you are likely to communicate this unconsciously to the aggressor and reduce the chances of an attack.

When you have calmed the person down keep focused on the problem and how you can help them resolve it

Be sympathetic and supportive and show you were listening by mentioning something they had previously mentioned.

Exercise

Now take fifteen minutes to discuss the points covered and which strategies are likely to apply most to your workplace.

Doing this as a team will allow you to build strategies for managing difficult situations that all of the staff team agree with and are aware of.

An Understanding of Anger and how it controls the mind of the aggressor

Anger is a primal emotion that is designed to defend you from perceived threats. It is an emotion run by the most primitive part of your brain, the amygdala.

As it is such a primitive response it bypasses conscious thought and puts your body into fight mode about quarter of a second before the conscious rational part of you has a say in what is going on.

Everyone has had the experience of this happening, like when you hear something just behind you so you spin around in surprise ready to defend yourself against whatever is there only to notice that it was a branch moving in the wind, casting a shadow, not a threat. In the time it took you to turn around you had consciously received enough information to make the decision that there was really no threat, so you calm down.

If when your mind assesses the information it still perceives a threat then it won't stop the aggressive response. That aggressive response will grow into a narrow, fixed focus of attention on what it is that you feel you need to defend against.

In the past that normally would have been physical dangers like Lions or other tribes invading your land. Nowadays it is more likely to be anger in defence of ideas or beliefs. As these are threats that won't go away unless your opinion changes the anger that starts has no new immediate information to stop it.

I say immediate because it is the information just after the aggression begins that causes the decision to carry on or to calm down. Any information after this is too late. The anger will have taken control until the threat is gone or has burnt itself out.

When the anger takes control you enter a highly focused state of mind. The more intelligent parts of your mind don't get accessed. This causes black or white thinking. It causes a state or mind where there is no grey. You are right they are wrong. It reduces your intelligence because your thinking doesn't have access to the more advanced communication centres of your brain.

It is for these reasons that you can't use many of the strategies that some other courses teach. You can't reason with the angry person because they will not see other points of view.

It is important to realise that the fight or flight response which is happening in the aggressive person is also happening in the person that is facing the aggression.

How you feel physically inside is also how the aggressor is feeling inside. The difference is how you are using these feelings and this response. Physically it is the same response whether you get scared and run or get angry and fight. Another option that can happen is that you can freeze. This is also a survival response. Many animals drop to the ground when they are attacked and 'play dead'. When for example the Lion that just chased down the gazelle has caught the gazelle, which collapses to the ground, the lion can then go and get her young before returning. In this brief window of opportunity the gazelle can get up, shake out the built up energy and run back to join its herd.

The physiological effects that you will both be experiencing are:

- When you experience fear or anger your body floods with stress hormones like adrenaline and noradrenalin
- You get a release of sugar and fat by the liver to increase the amount of energy in your body ready for fighting or running
- Breathing speeds up to give you more oxygen
- Blood rushes to the muscles in the arms and legs and to the brain to prepare you to run or stand and fight
- The heart speeds up and blood pressure rises to help ensure that oxygenated blood gets to where it is required
- Your muscles tense up as they prepare to be used
- Non essential bodily functions shut down, functions that are not necessary for immediate survival like digestion and saliva production. This can cause feelings of a dry mouth, butterflies in your stomach and loosening of the bowels and bladder

- Your senses become heightened and time can often seem to slow right down which allows you to make quick decisions or take rapid action
- Your pupils dilate which lets more light in allowing you to take in more information

Often after incidents have occurred these effects are still lingering and can make you feel uncomfortable and perhaps feeling like maybe you are having a panic attack. You are not. It is just the residual effects of these changes. If you shake yourself or do something active this can help to reduce the effects and calm you down. After an incident your body doesn't just instantly return to normal. It can take five to ten minutes to begin to feel calmer. The effects will last longer than this out of your awareness but your breathing and pulse will normally be more relaxed in that space of time.

The difference between aggression aimed at you and at others, and how to manage incidents

When aggression or violence is aimed at you it can feel quite intimidating. Often when you deal with aggression or violence that is aimed at others it feels easier to manage because it isn't an immediate threat to you. It doesn't create such a high emotional reaction.

For example; I had a situation when a young person in my care became threatening towards a pedestrian. He had a broken bottle and was threatening to stab the pedestrian. I stood in the way. Because he was being aggressive and was in a very focused anger trance aimed at the pedestrian it was as if I wasn't even there. I was standing with him leaning on me trying to get to the pedestrian. I didn't feel in any danger because none of the aggression was aimed at me.

The advantage of dealing with aggressive situations rather than having the aggression aimed at you is that you are already in a much calmer state. This allows you to make better decisions and to have more control over how you manage the situation.

Managing incidents of aggression or violence aimed at you, you need to first manage yourself. You need to keep calm and keep the logical part of your mind active.

If the aggression is aimed at others then unless the aggression turns onto you it can feel much easier to manage as you don't feel under so much threat so you can feel calmer and more relaxed and have clearer thoughts and the ability to make better decisions.

How to manage aggression aimed at others

Managing aggression aimed at others can often involve having to remove the main aggressor to start the calming down process. Sometimes you may remove the person on the receiving end of the aggression. For example you may remove a staff member that is on the receiving end of aggression by saying that they are wanted on the phone, and then you could take over helping the aggressor.

When you are dealing with aggression aimed at others it is often easier because you are often already calmer. You have to decide whether it is a better option to remove the aggressor or the victim from the situation to manage it effectively.

Often if there is more than one victim (like in a class room where many people are being disrupted by the aggressor) then it maybe preferable to remove the aggressor. Likewise, if you felt that you could move the aggressor successfully when there is only one victim or a few victims, then you could remove the aggressor.

If the aggression is aimed at others you are likely to be more clear headed so you are likely to be making better decisions. You don't want to go into the situation making judgmental comments. You may not know what has happened even if you think you know what you saw.

When aggression is aimed at others you need to act fast in an appropriate way. In situation that can quickly get out of control, like brawls, all it takes is for the victim to be pulled to the floor and they will then probably get seriously injured. Also nowadays, unfortunately, many people will join in the fight because they will think it will be fun.

You have to think about these things when you make your decision what course of action to take. If you get physically involved think about what consequences could occur, what you can do to help whilst maintaining your safety. It could be that you decided the only safe course of action.

You don't want to go getting physically involved when you can't effectively manage the situation. You may decide just calling the police is the only sensible option.

Assessing situations, maintaining safety

When you enter a situation with someone being aggressive it is important that you assess the situation as thoroughly as possible in your own mind. You need to know as much as you can about the aggressor and how they are likely to respond. If the aggressor is a client you may have information about them that can allow you to plan in advance how best to manage their behaviour. You need to know of any potential threats that could be present in the room like knives or scissors.

So many people fail to plan an adequate course of action in advance. Often I find that those that don't plan well say that it is because of the paperwork involved. In many lines of work like teaching, care work and nursing behavioural risk assessments need to be written down and often care plans for clients need to be written to include risks the client presents

Regardless of the line of work that you do you should write risk assessments on managing violence and aggression, these should identify the potential risks and strategies in place to reduce the possibility of the identified risks from occurring and, if the risk occurs then strategies for dealing with the situations.

To maintain safety it is important that you take notice of identified risks and don't do what might put you at increased risk. I have known of some staff that have put themselves at high levels of unnecessary risk even though the risk was identified and avoidable just because a manager has told them they don't have a choice.

Don't let anyone bully you into putting yourself at increased risk. In the situation above the manager didn't want to come on shift to cover a member of staff that hadn't turned up for work because they were sick. This meant that a member of staff was being told they were going to have to work alone in a situation that had a high chance of violence occurring. Risk assessments identified the risks but the manager wanted to ignore them.

The same situation has happened with me. The difference was that I refused to be left in a situation of increased risk when it was unnecessary. I made this clear to the manager. If they had left me in that situation and anything happened because of it they would have got into trouble for ignoring a risk assessment just so that they didn't have to work.

When you assess a situation some points you need to take into consideration:

- What potential weapons are available to the aggressor
- What is known about the aggressor, what is their history

- How many people are involved, how many of these are being aggressive or likely to be a threat
- Do you have back up
- Is there an escape route for you that you can get to before the aggressor

Deciding on a course of action

Whenever you enter a situation it is always useful to have a course of action in place. Often this course of action can be planned well in advance in staff meetings. It is important that all staff know what to do in various situations. For example it is important to have a plan of what staff will do in a shop if they suspect someone of planning on shoplifting. It could be that a plan is put in place that a member of staff will alert other staff to the suspect; this may put the plan into action that the staff member may approach the suspect; another member of staff may get by a phone or radio in case the police are required. It may be planned that the staff member that approaches the suspect will just ask if they want a basket for the goods they have.

Any common or likely situations that may occur in your workplace should be planned for so that everyone in the workplace knows what to do. In care work you know the history of clients and you have ongoing behaviour management plans that you should be discussing and updating on a weekly or fortnightly basis. These behaviour management plans allow you and any new staff to come on shift and know what to do in a wide variety of situations. They should also identify whether people are likely to work as a gang or have a few bullying an individual or only aggressive alone. Also how they respond to aggressive or violent situations going on around them.

In care work especially it is important to know if any client is likely to get violent or join in violence when another client gets aggressive. So many situations I have seen where staff go to deal with a situation only to find that they are then attacked by a resident that was calm but got aggressive because of the situation going on.

This attack when unexpected has a high risk of someone getting seriously injured. The same can happen when fights occur involving the public, for example outside nightclubs or in hospitals where one person may be violent and whilst staff are managing the situation others may get involved 'just for fun'.

How you feel that you can manage the situation will effect what course of action you will decide on. It could be that you feel that too many people are about that look like they will join in so you feel it would be unsafe to physically get involved but that calling for back up and calling the police would be the best course of action.

You may decide that because you have to deal with a situation alone you will keep distance and just call the police. You may have a few colleagues with you and so feel that you could all manage the situation and separate the aggressor to somewhere quieter to calm them down.

Don't go into a situation with no idea what you will do. People make mistakes, sometimes things don't work out as expected, that's just the way things are. But it is important that you at least have a plan of action. You need to know what you are confident dealing with, what back up you will have. As mentioned earlier in this book, taking no action can be seen as being negligent. If you feel that you can't manage the situation then make your course of action to call the police. If you need more staff but feel that between you, you can manage the situation then get more staff first. What is important is that you DO SOMETHING.

Having more than one staff member involved even if the other staff member(s) are just witnesses

Whenever a staff member goes into a violent or aggressive situation or a situation that has the potential to turn more aggressive they should always have another staff member involved. This other staff member may just be someone that is nearby to hear what is going on, or it may be a case of just telling someone where you are going or what you are doing and when you will be back.

For example in care work it is always important to say what you are doing at all times. If you are going up stairs to a client's room you need to tell another staff member that that is what you are doing and that you will be back in five minutes or however long you expect to be. If you don't do this and something happens to you when you go to the room no one will come looking for you. They may just assume you are in the office doing paperwork.

Always make sure people know what you are doing, where you are going to be and how long for, even if it is just to go to the toilet.

If you do social work make sure that you tell someone that you will call them at the time the appointment is due to finish in a client's house. Make sure that someone also knows your location. If you don't call them then they will know that something may be wrong. In a hospital, make sure that other staff know what you are doing and where you will be. You may have to go into specific sealed wards or into situations with people where you will be isolated. Perhaps you may have to go and get something from a storeroom, even this you should tell someone, what if you were followed?

Remember never mind how confident you are, and how sure you are that nothing will happen to you it may do, so be prepared and work as a team.

Exercise

Take some time to discuss what has been covered so far and what possible aggressive, violent or confrontational situations you could make a plan for in your workplace. This could begin to become a basis for an ongoing violence and aggression risk assessment and action plan.

Think of all the possible risks, in detail, never mind how small or unlikely they seem. For example if you worked in care for people with mental health issues, you could include issues surrounding medication (like not taking it, changes to it, side effects).

If you worked in childcare you could include issues like drug dealers or gangs arriving at the home you work in or being met in the streets while the child is in your care.

If you work in domestic violence you could include partners becoming aggressive with you.

If you work in elderly care homes it could be an aggressive son or daughter of a resident that feels the care isn't of a high enough standard and so attacks you.

In retail shops it could be customer's trying to shoplift then becoming aggressive. In nightclubs it could be drunken gangs. In schools it could be a violent pupil or parent. In restaurants it could be a customer irritated with the wait that gets violent.

Whatever your sector there will be situations that could arise involving violence or aggression that will be handled more confidently and most likely more effectively if the situation was well planned for in advance.

The importance of having an awareness of the aggressors basic emotional needs

If you have an awareness of the basic emotional needs that people have you can begin to know what situations are likely to be most conducive to causing an increase of violence or aggression and what situations are likely to reduce violence or aggression, or even lead to a calmer environment.

By being aware of the needs of the aggressor you may find it quicker and easier to know what needs to change or happen to resolve situations. Likewise if you are aware of the basic emotional needs you can notice what needs to change to make the environment or situation better for the staff.

Staff work better, more productively and have a higher tolerance to stress when their emotional needs are being met appropriately.

The same applies for the aggressor; if their personal needs are all met appropriately then they are not likely to get aggressive.

The basic human needs are:

1. The need to give and receive attention

We all have a need to get a certain level of attention. If someone feels that they are not getting enough attention then there is an increased chance of that person being involved negatively in situations. It could be that they are a member of staff that feels ignored so has a lower tolerance to other colleagues and snaps at them more. Or it could be a customer or client that has personal problems that include receiving a lack of attention or that is sat in a waiting room with no-one acknowledging them so they feel they are being ignored, which could lead to an incident. Any lack of attention can lead to a craving for the attention or a despair due to not having the attention, some people will begin to change character and play up and may even become aggressive, while others will change and get withdrawn.

2. The mind body connection

If anyone gets reduced sleep or reduced exercise they are likely to become more mentally lethargic and more prone to stress and anger. They are likely to snap more due to having less tolerance.

If on the other hand anyone is happy for some reason or kept jolly or laughing then they are likely to be more stress free and more tolerant to others around them. They will appear far more capable of coping.

Also the more stressed people get the less tolerance they have to physical pain and at the same time the more chance they have of suffering aches and pains and headaches. Whereas a relaxed person will be more tolerant to pain, they will also be less likely to experience pain.

This can make a huge difference in hospitals and A & E especially where people already are likely to be experiencing some level of discomfort and so by keeping them relaxed they will be more able to calmly manage their discomfort rather than becoming angry.

3. The need for purpose and goals

Everybody has a need for purpose and goals. Not just for the rewards specifically but because we are all hardwired to need a purpose and to want things to achieve. Many customers or clients that are aggressive will have a purpose or an agenda set out that they plan on following. Normally when people complain they have spent time planning in their mind.

People that remain most 'sane' are the ones that can break down a goal to having an outcome each day (or more often). This allows them to always feel in control of their destiny and it gives their life meaning.

It can be possible to help some people that are being aggressive by helping them to find a reason for not carrying out the behaviour they are doing. It maybe that they have had a really bad few months and are feeling depressed and have now become aggressive in retaliation to a perceived threat. It may be possible to listen to the person and to look out for things they say without realising it, that imply a purpose they could follow.

There is a Simpson's episode where Homer tries to kill himself, he ties a boulder to himself and is going to through himself off a bridge when an accident nearly happens and Homer realises that if there was a road sign then it would make the road safe. He then decides he doesn't want to commit suicide, he has to make Springfield safe.

4. Connection to something bigger than yourself

It is a human trait that we want a connection to something bigger than ourselves (whether a religion or a group or a cause). Work colleagues are likely to form groups and then class themselves as belonging to a group. This will serve many purposes' including to meet many of these needs. If anyone becomes outcast they are likely to become emotional and feel they don't belong. This can lead to a depressed mood, resentment and anger. Often groups will not talk enough with each other and small issues will be blown out of proportion with groups blaming each other with the groups all thinking in a black and white style (I'm right, you're wrong, no in-between or grey).

This is one reason why teams should always have regular meeting and air any issues. Often most issues are misunderstandings, something has been heard from someone else and this has spread. If you work in care then your residents should all also have regular house meetings. This is especially the case if there is a chance of certain residents forming groups against other residents.

You should also look out for situations where clients might form gangs and where they might target another client or a staff member. If they do target a staff member then this needs to be addressed with the other staff about how best to manage the situation.

When groups form that exclude anyone (like can happen in care home situations and sometimes between work colleagues) there is a possibility that it may lead to bullying, which obviously is also increasing the chances of aggressive or violent situations arising.

5. **The need for stimulation and creativity**

Again as us humans are hardwired with a need for stimulation and creativity, if this is denied it is likely to lead to boredom, anxiety and stress. In situations where not a lot happens and boredom can set in easily people may create games to play to meet this need or begin drinking lots of tea or coffee, or smoking more than normal to try to get some stimulation of any kind.

6. The need to feel understood and connected

If people get along this need gets met. If they form small groups those in the groups are likely to get this need met. If on the other hand anyone isn't in a group and doesn't get on with anyone they are likely to quickly get quite down and appear to be quite low.

If this need isn't met, for example; if someone (like a therapist's client) tries to explain how they feel and tries to talk to the therapist but doesn't get the help they are expecting then they may begin feeling that they have been rejected, and that no-one understands them.

There are many situations in which people feel they are not being listened to or understood. This can make the person even angrier. The best course of action to take is to do your best to appear as helpful as possible.

Agree with the person as much as possible and if you have to disagree avoid saying things like 'yes, but…' as this makes people defensive.

7. The need to feel a sense of control

A sense of control is vital to all of us. In many situations unfortunately most of the control is taken away. If someone is waiting in a queue, they have no control over how quickly the queue moves or how well the staff are working; the same applies to people waiting in hospitals or A & E. In care homes the staff are the ones that set the boundaries so they take away a level of control, on the roads you can't control other road users. On public transport you can't control delays.

People will try to give themselves control in their own ways. They may have group ways of having control. They may develop rituals (like saying something before eating at meals, or arranging things in a specific way). People that will cope best are likely to create control in their mind. This is what POW's often do to survive. They will count to a given number before screaming, etc…

The best way to manage situations and avoid aggression is to at least give the illusion of control to the people. it could be the employer giving a few options for staff to choose between, or the care staff offering a few choices of snack to the children before they go to bed, or asking if they want to be woken at 0715 or 0730 in the morning and if they want a drink brought to their room when they wake up.

There are many ways to offer choices or find something a person has control over in a situation. If someone feels they have no control they may get aggressive, so help them to have control.

When I used to work in childcare as a sanction for not getting up in time in the morning I would sometimes tell the child that if they didn't get up in fifteen minutes they would have their television removed from their room until they can show that they can get up on time three days in a row (I would have asked them to get up a number of times by this stage).

This sanction puts control on the child. If they get up they don't lose their television, if they don't get up they lose their television but can get it back in as little as three days. Or they could lose their television for longer if they continue to not get up. The choice is theirs, they are in control. The staff also win because the child has to learn to get up on time to get their television back and they also show that boundaries will be put in place and carried out.

What is necessary to remember when confronted with aggression or violence

Control over yourself

It is important that you have control over yourself. When you are in an aggressive situation it is all too easy to begin to feel out of control. What you need to do is to learn how to step back in your mind and relax. Begin to take control of your breathing and how you are acting.

Learn to do 3 – 5 breathing. This is where you breathe in to the count of 3 and out to the count of 5. What this does is it sets off the relaxation response. It can also be useful to consciously let your shoulders relax.

Control how you respond before any incident even begins. So many staff say things that can be overheard causing the situation to escalate or due to their expectations the situation goes how it is expected to go.

For example:

Saying 'here she comes, better prepare yourself for trouble'

Or

'He never settles on time, it always leads to a restraint'

Clearly if you have an attitude that things will go wrong or if you say things that can be overheard there is an increased chance of those things happening.

Don't take anything personally

When someone is being aggressive towards you they don't really know what they are saying. They have an agenda. They are fighting for what at that time they believe to be right.

Part of this fighting maybe to attack you verbally.

If you start to take what is said to you personally then you are likely to begin to get annoyed and aggressive also. What you need to do is understand that it doesn't matter what is said to you.

I have heard so many times people, including myself being told that 'my mother is an fucking whore' or 'I'm going to follow you home and kill you and your partner' or 'I'm going to fuck your wife'. It is important to remain calm and just focus on the situation at hand. It doesn't matter what is said to you or about you.

Often if the aggressive person is complaining they may aim all of their aggression and all of the blame at you because you are the person that happens to be on the desk at the time.

The aggressor has probably spent a while 'psyching' themselves up to complain. They have probably gone over and over what is going to happen and what they want to say in their mind dozens of times so the best thing to do is to let them get it off their chest without taking any of it personally and without interrupting them or saying that they are wrong.

Awareness of your surroundings

Within your workplace you should always be aware of your surroundings. So often people get harmed by objects that they or other colleagues have left lying around, or they put themselves in positions of increased risk.

It could be that in a care home for young people you are cooking and using a sharp knife. Just then a young person comes into the kitchen being aggressive.

The sensible thing to do would be to calmly put the knife somewhere out of sight, but so often I have known of people to just put the knife down on the side as they turn around to deal with the situation.

Unfortunately in doing this you leave a potentially lethal weapon in view that the aggressor could pick up and use. The same sort of thing could happen in any number of situations, for example, leaving a sharp pair of scissors on the counter when talking with an angry customer in a shop, or leaving scalpels or other sharp objects in reach within a hospital environment.

All of these objects should be put out of sight to reduce the risk of having them used aggressively.

Staff often unwittingly put themselves into situations without much thought for safety. It could be a doctor working in an office that puts the desk across the room from the door. This means that you are putting yourself at risk if someone comes into the office and gets aggressive because they will be positioned between you and the escape route.

The ideal position for the desk would be to have the desk in a corner near the door so that once the client has sat down if they get aggressive you are closer to the door than they are. (See diagram below)

By having an awareness of your surroundings you can begin to reduce unnecessary risks.

```
         Desk
Doctor          Patient


Door to the room
```

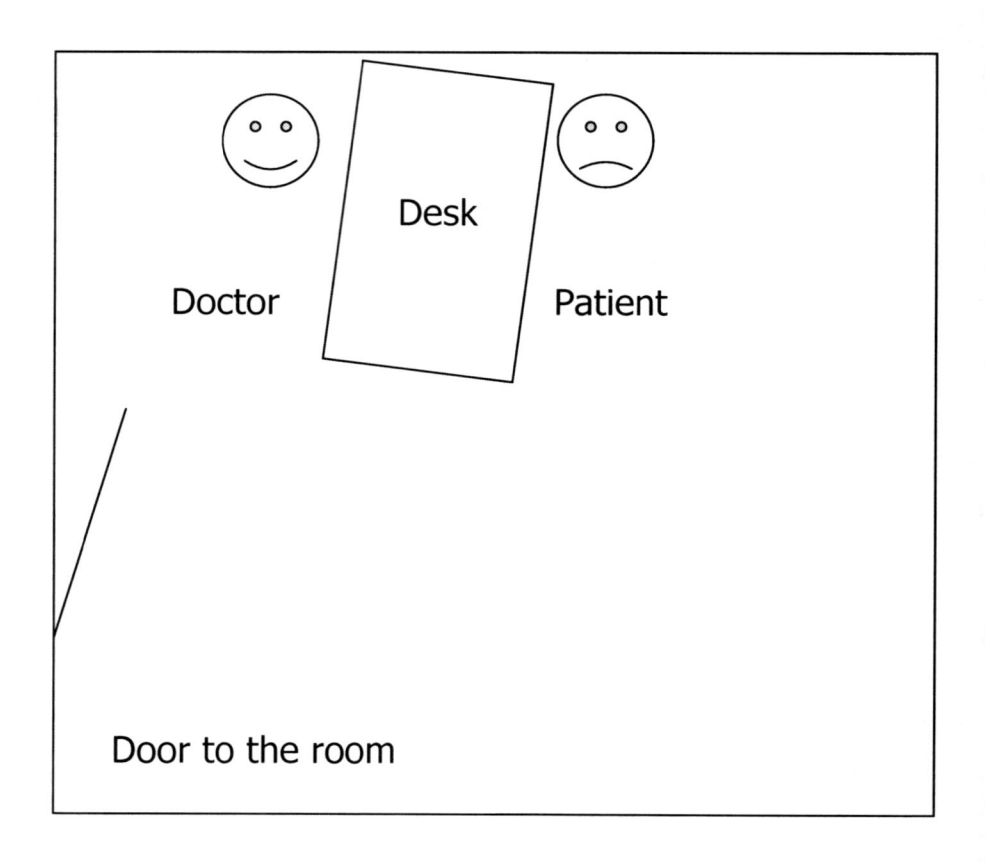

Don't take unnecessary risks or be complacent, trust evidence that is presented to you. There are often reports of social workers that go to see patients in their homes and even though the patient has a history of violence they will think it will never happen to them, or they feel uncomfortable at the house yet still enter then get attacked.

There was plenty of evidence it just got ignored. For situations like this it is important to have risk assessments in place and to have an action plan in place about what needs to happen to reduce the risk.

If, for example, the social worker has no choice but to enter the situation alone then perhaps it is decided that they will call to alert someone of their arrival and will agree that they will only stay in the house for thirty minutes then will call someone again to let them know that they have come out of the house and are alright.

It is better to be cautious and safe than take risks and be dead.

Forward Planning

Hindsight is a wonderfully useful thing so why not start with it. If you plan in advance how you will respond in situations or what various outcomes are possible and what might cause problems to occur you can reduce risks and plan better ways of managing situations.

For example, you can plan

- Exits, how you are going to get out from situations
- Staff changeovers, how you can make them run more smoothly with the least amount of disruption to other people. Often it is situations like staff changeovers that cause many people to become angry because they see all these staff holding up queues in supermarkets as they finish their shifts, or in care homes most of the staff disappear to the office to hand over as a new shift comes on. This leaves too few staff dealing with the client group and also causes many clients to want to know what is being discussed in the office as most get paranoid about being talked about.

Exercise

Practice 3 – 5 breathing. Counting in to the count of 3 and out to the count of 5. Begin to notice how you start to feel relaxed. As you do the 3 – 5 breathing make sure that you breathe from deep down in your chest. To relax more you can also consciously let your shoulders slump and relax.

After you have done that spend some time discussing what in your working environment could be used as an aggressive implement and how you could reduce the risk.

Also discuss whether there are any situations in your work place that could have risk reduced, for example by situating a desk so that you have quick access to an exit that doesn't pass an aggressor, or planning to call a colleague at set times if out seeing a client, or planning staff change over's to reduce the impact that they have on customers or clients.

Discuss how you can reduce any identified risks. It maybe useful to write these things down on a board so that as a team you can come back to them in the future to readdress them if necessary.

Non-physical strategies for managing aggression or its onset

The idea of these strategies is to avoid the situation leading to aggression. Ideally you want to do what you can to avoid a situation getting physical so it is useful to have a number of learnt skills and techniques.

Before moving onto the physical strategies for managing aggression I am going to cover a number of non-physical strategies.

The idea of these strategies is to avoid the situation leading to aggression.

Offering support, when someone is beginning to get frustrated

Often when people are beginning to get frustrated it can help to offer support. Offering support can make the aggressor feel calmer as they can feel that you are working with them not against them.

When you offer support it is best to try to both sit down to talk. This will help to calm the situation down, as sitting is a calming action whereas standing is more active. You can start by feeding back what the aggressor says to show understanding.

Distraction

Distraction is a useful way of stopping the build up of aggression. Everyone has had the experience of having something on their mind that they are about to say and just as they go to say it someone cuts in and says something else or they say something like 'hang on a minute I've just got to do this'. And when they ask you what you wanted to say you find that you have forgotten.

In a care home perhaps the distraction could be that you say you thought you just heard a knock at the door. If it was in a shop perhaps you could say that you just have to take some items to the checkout then you will be right back. If it is in a hospital you may say that you will just go and see if you can find out further information and that you will be back in a minute.

To use distraction effectively it works best to be a non-threatening distraction and one that the aggressor would be happy to accept. It also works best if you do it by timing an interruption well.

Reassurance that you will do what you can

Offering reassurance to someone that is becoming aggressive is a useful technique for seeming to come alongside the aggressor and show that you will do your best to sort out their situation. Often even if you fail to resolve the situation the fact that they have seen that you tried your best will lead to the aggressor thanking you for your help.

Planned ignoring like walking away with a reason

When someone is angry they are very focused and one-minded. This means that they don't always listen or see alternative points of view. If you take yourself out of a situation leaving the aggressor alone in the situation they have no one to be angry with and so if it is done correctly the aggressor will begin to calm down.

When the aggressor is calm enough they will be more likely to listen to what you have to say.

Planned ignoring works well with children, young people and adults alike. What you need to do is to give the aggressor a legitimate sounding reason for why you need to walk away and a time frame for when you will return. This is important because then the aggressor shouldn't get worked up that you have been gone for ages until the time you said has passed.

Reason that you could give could be things like saying 'I'll just go and check to see why you have been kept waiting so long, I'll be back in a few minutes.' or 'I just need to make a call to find out more information, it should only take a few minutes'.

In childcare planned ignoring is a key strategy to use whether it is saying 'I'm just going to the other room to give you time to calm down. I'll come back in five minutes to see how calm you are' or whether you say something like 'I've just got to make a quick call then I'll be straight back. It should only take about five minutes'.

With children and young people it is important that you make them aware that you will talk to them when they talk to you calmly and not when they are shouting, swearing and demanding from you. There are times when you may let swearing slide a little for example when they have received bad news and are angry and not in control of what they are saying.

If you try to stop them swearing then it won't work. You need to show you are listening and use other strategies and when they have calmed enough to respond to you then you can mention not swearing.

Planned ignoring based on the behaviour when the child or young person is in a high state of anger is less likely to work than giving an excuse to temporarily remove yourself from the situation.

Removing an audience

Removing an audience helps to calm down situations with adults, young people and children. With adults having an audience often makes them feel more uncomfortable which in turn can increase their level of aggression. With children and young people if there is an audience they are more likely to play up to it so by removing the audience they are likely to calm down more.

Removing the audience can be done in two ways; firstly it can be done by having everyone moving from the situation. This option works fine when the audience is in a care home and consists of staff and residents because you can have the staff say to the residents something like, 'why don't we go to the lounge and get ready to watch the film'. And they can work together to all move from the current room.

In somewhere like a shop or hospital or surgery or school classroom this option is not so easy to do. In those situations what is needed is to remove the aggressor away from the audience. This has the same result of removing the audience.

To do this you could just simply suggest it, like saying, 'why don't we move to the other room. It's a little quieter in there so we can talk properly', or 'why don't we go just round the corner to get out of the noise. Then I can pay you my full attention'.

Sometimes, depending on your line of work it may be necessary to remove the aggressor physically from a situation like perhaps removing a disruptive child from a classroom in school.

Offering some time to calm down

Sometimes it can be useful to offer some time to someone to allow them to calm down before talking with them. When people calm down they begin to see more rationally.

If you are going to offer time for someone to calm down remember to say how long you will be away while they are calming or where they can find you when they are calmer.

This is a technique that works well for children. Giving them time to calm down before you will talk with them.

It could be that you suggest they sit in a room perhaps like the dining room to calm down.

It is important when working with children or young people not to send them to their own room because they will build the association between being worked up and being in their room.

You want them to associate calming and sleeping with their own bedroom.

Choices

Whenever you create choices in the mind of the aggressor you start breaking down the anger trance. This is because the angry person is in a focused state of mind and only sees black and white. By creating choices in their mind you start creating greys this brings the rational part of the mind back into play which starts to dissolve the anger.

Choices often aren't readily taken on board when offered to someone that is highly aggressive but it does work well to start to prevent anger from continually escalating.

It could be that you offer a different meaning to the situation, for example if someone driving was angry with a car that just overtook them as a passenger you may say it looked like the woman in that car was pregnant. Even if this isn't true by offering that option the driver may then think that they can understand why the driver overtook.

It could be that you see someone that you suspect maybe planning on shoplifting. You could approach them an offer them a basket to carry what they have hidden. In doing this you have offered them choices. They now know you have seen them; they can now get out of the situation without any trouble and without your stock.

They now know that as they have been spotted if they try to carry out the shoplifting they will be stopped and perhaps prosecuted. If on the other hand you didn't offer them choices and you decided to stop them just after they have left the shop they have no good options, either they fight for freedom or get caught.

Sometimes if you know what you are doing you can offer highly aggressive people choices that stop them in their tracks and snap them out of the anger trance and make them have to see the options presented.

For example, I had this incident where a young person in my care was being violent. He had Stanley knife blades on him with one of them in his hand. He said he would cut anyone that approached him. He was in the lounge so I went into the lounge.

I didn't know why he was so angry, I told him 'if you really want to hurt me there isn't much I can do to stop you, what I want to do is talk to you to see how I can help you, so I am going to sit down in this chair here. If you want to get angry with me then that's up to you, if you want to talk to me so that I know what is wrong and if I can help then you can do that.'

This shocked him out of his anger trance because the response he expected to the threat was for everyone to back away and be intimidated. I wasn't intimidated and I didn't feel I was at risk. If I felt I couldn't handle the situation I wouldn't have done what I did.

By offering an option to talk without getting in trouble he had a way out. Until I spoke to him all that was in his mind was either the staff move away and he could then get out of the house to get rid of the blades, or we go to hold him and to get the blades which would have increased the aggression.

By sitting down and being non-threatening and offering choices without mentioning the blades he calmed down and after he was calm and had spoken he was also in a state of mind to be asked for the blades and to know we needed them from him.

Negotiating

Another strategy is negotiating with the aggressor before they become too aggressive. Being prepared to perhaps compromise like maybe if you worked with children, rather than demand that they clean their room and have them continue to argue and get more aggressive about not wanting to, you could offer to help them.

Setting boundaries

Is a strategy to use with children and young people. By having boundaries in place that are all agreed and stuck to by all of the staff team the children know what they can and can't do. If there have been no boundaries in place then to start with the children may become more challenging as they try to fight against the new boundaries.

After a short period of time the children will be used to the boundaries and will accept them. Without boundaries children may be difficult at bedtimes and not settle they may ignore everything that they are told. It is important that any response to broken boundaries doesn't remove choices.

For example, I have known of staff that tell the child that because they don't get up in the morning they are having their television removed from their room for a week.

The problem with this sanction is that the child can now stay in bed all week without losing anything. A better way of doing a similar sanction is to tell the child that the television is being removed because they haven't been getting up in the morning and they can have it back when they get up on time three days in a row.

This immediately puts control in the hands of the child. They could have the TV back in three days or continue to not get up and so not get their TV back for weeks. Either way the choice is theirs. This keeps an incentive to get up each morning even though they have had their TV removed.

Changing the staff member

Sometimes people being aggressive may be aiming all of their anger at a specific staff member. In these situations it can be useful to find a way of changing staff members. This also works to cause a little distraction.

You could do this by either saying that you will get someone that may be of more help, or if you see someone in that situation perhaps you go over and tell the staff member they are wanted on the phone and that you will take over.

Maintaining or setting routines

Routines are important for aiding stability. When people don't have a set routine they can begin to feel uncomfortable because they feel a lack of security and structure. In childcare especially children are much calmer when they receive meals at regular time and get woken and go to bed at regular times.

By creating regular routines you will minimise anger build up. This works just as well with staff. When staff know times of breaks and shift patterns and have a plan for the shift they feel calmer. Whereas if there is no routine for staff they have times on shift where they don't know what they should be doing or when their breaks will be which can cause staff to feel out of control of what they should be doing.

This feeling can be increased if there is also uncertainty around shifts and not knowing from week to week when you will be working because this limits how much staff can plan their personal lives so often they can begin to resent their work because they can feel that it is impacting too much on their personal life.

Major life threatening situations like when weapons are used

For major life threatening situations like if someone is punching or kicking at you or if they have weapons like a knife, then the best course of action is to get help. Shout stating exactly what is going on and get something between you and the aggressor if you can't get out of the situation. It could be that you get behind a desk or that you get a chair between you and the aggressor.

If the worst comes to the worst you can use reasonable force to defend yourself which could involve hitting them hard in the legs with a chair or doing some other move to defend yourself. As long as you feel that it was all you could do to save yourself then there shouldn't be a problem with justifying what you did. It is better to face a jury and be alive than not defend yourself and be dead.

I always advise getting out of situations as quick as possible, but there are times when you maybe confronted with an aggressor brandishing a weapon and have no alternative but to face them.

In these situations I am going to give a few basic guidelines. Remember I always recommend getting out of the situation and trying to avoid doing anything you don't feel confident doing, but I also understand that it is better to have a few pointers on dealing with weapons than no advice at all.

If someone attacks you with a gun you want to get away from them as fast as you can, you also want to be moving. The important thing is to be a difficult target to hit. Go behind objects like tables and chairs. These won't shield you effectively but will make the target (you) smaller.

Remember the point is to give yourself the few seconds needed to get out of the situation (assuming this is possible).

The other option is, if it isn't going to point the gun at anyone else, to get in close to the aggressor grabbing the gun from the side and turning your body so that it is completely out of line of fire and getting the gun to the floor perhaps by putting all of your weight onto the gun. If you are out of the line of fire then even if it goes off, if you are doing one quick movement then the gun will be forced to the ground without you getting shot.

The important thing is to weigh up the risks, generally the higher the risk of getting seriously injured or killed the more likely you are to try higher risk strategies, as doing nothing will get you shot.

If someone attacks you with a weapon they are swinging, like a baseball bat, or a cricket bat, or a snooker cue, or any other weapon normally around a metre long, or longer. What you need to do is get in close to the aggressor. Usually the aggressor will be holding the weapon in two hands. This makes them easier to manage because they are likely to be focused on using the weapon rather than kicking or head-butting, etc.

Ideally you want to charge in close as they swing the weapon backwards just before they are about to strike. At this point they will leave their whole body open and vulnerable. When you get in close you will need to take them down rapidly to maintain your safety. Ways that you can do this are, aiming for the groin, aiming for the throat, or aiming for the bottom of the rib cage in the centre of the body.

The reason why you move in close is because the most powerful part of the swing is when the end of the object hits you, so if you keep trying to avoid being hit eventually you are likely to be, and when you are it could be serious or fatal. The aggressor can't swing properly when you are up close to them and being hit is likely to be far less powerful.

If someone attacks you with a knife you want to get distance. Knives are probably the most fatal of all the major weapons likely to face the average worker. You don't want to get into a wrestling match over the knife as someone is likely to get seriously hurt. One advantage you do have, like you do with anyone that is using a weapon, is that they are likely to focus their attack on involving the weapon which limits what they are likely to do.

If you can grab the aggressor by the wrist of the hand holding the weapon and put another hand up by their shoulder, you can twist them to the ground with the hand holding the knife stretched out whilst they are then laying face down on the ground. From this position you have a better chance of controlling the aggressor, unarmed.

Other options are to get an object in the way like holding a chair that can stop the aggressor being able to stab you. Or a possible last resort action could be to pick up a table (like classroom tables, or another table that is light enough to pick up) and to charge at them with the top of the table facing them, keeping enough distance between the rear of the table and your body (as the knife may penetrate the table), pushing them to a wall. This may cause them some harm if done hard, but the chances are the knife will either get dropped or stuck in the table.

As a last resort this could be effective in stopping the aggressor and disarming them.

There are obviously many other potential situations and solutions, and many solutions that are specific to your workplace and different locations in your workplace. For example I have previously mentioned how I had to shut a door on someone's arm as they lunged a piece of broken mirror at my face.

In all areas of your workplace (all the different rooms etc) discuss as a team, room by room what you could do to deal with life threatening situations. What escapes routes do you have, what could be used to put between yourself and the aggressor. Discuss what you think you are likely to do. Make up scenarios then find ways of dealing with them.

Bullying

Bullying or people 'ganging up' is a common occurrence, especially within care homes. It also happens within small staff teams.

Unfortunately it is easy for people to get sucked into conversations and to begin to focus their attention on the ideas of the group; this is one way that people form bonds. They share mutual beliefs and views.

The same thing happens everywhere. In workplaces where people work entirely separate shifts, rather than talk to the people on the other shifts they form an idea based on gossip led by the people with the strongest views and most out spoken. Over a short period of time they turn against staff on other shifts creating a 'them and us' culture.

Once your attention is focused on something it becomes difficult not to notice it. For example; I was ran over by a Nissan Nivara. I never recalled really noticing one on the roads beforehand but as soon as I was out of hospital and back walking the streets it seemed that I would be passed by about 6 – 10 each day.

They didn't just suddenly appear over night, they had been there for sometime but all of a sudden my attention was focused on noticing them, just like any habits that people have that began to really aggravate someone into becoming aggressive, often if it is workplace violence or aggression whether between staff or between residents or patients, those habits where often always there, it's just that the persons attention has become more focused on noticing those habits.

Bullying is specific. Bullying involves having one person being singled out and targeted for who they specifically are (or something specific about them). Whereas racism is more general, everyone in the race is tarred with the same brush.

Obviously people can be bullied based on race but normally if this is the case the bullies would use terms to imply this by making generalised statements like saying 'they' rather than 'he'. As time goes on people begin to generalise, so what can start off as not liking one person can end up saying that everyone is the same.

For example; I have worked with women that had had abusive partners. In most cases those that endured the abuse from the partner for sometime had formed the opinion that 'all men are like that' which clearly isn't true; there are many decent men out there that would never be abusive.

Small groups can often share a view or belief that allows them to all fit in together. This meets many of their basic needs. They all get attention, they all get reassurance and support from the other group members, and they feel part of something bigger than themselves because they have a united belief and can support the other gang members.

Having a shared view allows them to feel connected to each other and can be quite intimate if it leads to sharing secrets and trusting each other. They get their need for stimulation and creativity met by plotting and theorising and discussing the person they are bullying, it gives them something to discuss. They are also likely to get a 'buzz' and a feeling of excitement from doing something wrong and from having confrontations (whether directly or being in the background but part of the confrontation). This happens because they will get an adrenaline rush, just like people get when they do extreme sports (which is the main reason many people do extreme sports).

If you work in care or in a situation where groups of people spend lots of time together (like pupils in schools, long term patients in hospitals, residential care homes, regular clubs, etc) you can pay attention to the subtle onset of bullying and begin to notice what role various individuals play in the process. You can watch for groups forming and group beliefs and views forming. You can watch for signs that a group is beginning to select a target and what caused them to choose that target (sometimes there is an event that someone isn't happy with that gets the group talking and then it spirals into bullying).

By observing these different factors you can discuss as a staff team ways to manage the situation to prevent aggression or violence from occurring.

Finally

Finally it is important that you work as a team and back each other when you are managing situations. The only time not to is if someone is doing something they shouldn't like hurting the aggressor or getting rough with them because they are getting angry also.

Any issues you have with how a situation was handled can be discussed afterwards. Often staff feel that a situation could have been handled differently so it is important that you talk about this.

After an incident everyone should support fellow staff members, it could be just checking they are alright or actually sitting down and talking the incident through. If you work in care or in schools or if the aggressor is a client or patient it is important that you also make time to talk to the aggressor and to help them move on after the incident, they should also be asked if they want to see a Doctor.

All recording, reporting needs to be done fully to show the duration of the incident and any holding that took place, any injuries need to be reported and recorded, what techniques were done need to be mentioned and who did what, right down to the details like who held which arm (For example if a restraint took place). If possible the opinions of all involved should be written down including the aggressor's views if it is appropriate. In your workplace you will have your own sets of standards that have to be adhered to.

As much accurate detail as possible should always be written down and all staff should regularly discuss in meetings what procedures should be followed. Staff meetings are a vital place for making sure that everyone knows what to do in the event of any incident, whether it is in the case of fire, health and safety, first aid, or violence and aggression.

This book has aimed to give you an understanding and knowledge of skills and techniques available to you to manage a wide range of situations and in a wide range of workplaces. As a staff team you should take what you have learnt and expand on it and adapt it to suit your specific place of work and specific situations.

Bibliography

Alder Harry & Heather Beryl, NLP in 21 days, Piatkus Publishers Ltd, 1999

Andreas Steve, Faulkner Charles, NLP: The New technology for Achievement, Nicholas Brealey, 1994

Bandler Richard & Grinder John, The structure of magic Vol. 1, Science & Behaviour Books Inc, 1975

Bandler Richard & Grinder John, The structure of magic Vol. 2, Science & Behaviour Books Inc, 1976

Bandler Richard, Magic in Action, Meta Publications, 1990

Bandler Richard, McDonald Will, An Insiders Guide to Sub Modalities, Meta Publications, 1988

Bandler Richard, State of the Art, Videos, McKenna Training, 1998

Bandler Richard, The Bandler Effect, DVD's, McKenna Training, 2005

Bandler Richard, Time for a Change, Meta Publications, 1993

Bandler Richard, Your Own Personal Genius, CD's, McKenna Training, 2001

Beattie Geoffrey, Visible thought, Routledge, 2003

Bolstad Richard, Resolve, Video, Transformations, 2001

Brooks Michael, Instant rapport, Warner Business Books, 1989

Brooks Stephen, Intensive Training in NLP & Ericksonian Hypnosis, CD's, Lawrence Enterprises, 1997

Brooks Stephen, The art of indirect hypnosis and minimal therapy, www.british-hypnosis-research.com

Brooks Stephen, The Art of Indirect Suggestion, CD's, Lawrence Enterprises, 1995

Brooks Stephen, Training in indirect hypnosis, www.british-hypnosis-research.com

Cameron-Bandler Leslie & LeBeau Michael, NLP home study guide, NLP Comprehensive, 1984

Claxton Guy, Hare Brain Tortoise Mind, Fourth Estate, 1998

Dawes Mark, Winn Denise, Managing the Monkey, The Therapist, 1999

Griffin Joe, Tyrrell Ivan, How to Master Anxiety, HG Publishing, 2007

Griffin Joe, Tyrrell Ivan, Freedom from Addiction, HG Publishing, 2005

Griffin Joe & Tyrrell Ivan, Human Givens, Human Givens Publishing, 2003

Griffin Joe, Effective Anger Management, Tape, ETSI, 2002

Griffin Joe, Understanding & Treating Addictions, Tape, ETSI, 2001

Hartmann Thom, Healing ADD, Underwood Books, 1998

Havens Ronald, The Wisdom of Milton H. Erickson, Crown House Publishing, 2003

Leeson Nick, Tyrrell Ivan, Back from the Brink, Virgin Books, 2005

Martin Paul, The Sickening Mind, Flamingo, 1997

O'Connor & Seymour John, Introducing NLP, Thorsons, 1990

O'Hanlon Bill & Beadle Sandy, A guide to possibility land, W. W. Norton & Co. 1999

O'Connor Joseph, NLP Workbook, Thorsons, 2001

O'Hanlon Bill & Weiner-Davis Michele, In search of solutions, W. W. Norton & Co. 1989

O'Hanlon Bill, Martin Michael, Solution-oriented Hypnosis, W.W. Norton & Co. 1992

Richardson Jerry, The magic of rapport, Meta Publications, 2000

Rossi Ernest, The 20 Minute Break, Tarcher, 1991

Watzlawick & Weakland & Fisch, Change, W. W. Norton & Co. 1974

Watzlawick Paul, The language of change, W. W. Norton & Co. 1993

Index

'fight or flight', 19, 36

3 – 5 breathing, 87, 94

A & E, 79, 84

abuse, 119

action plan, 45, 74, 93

action plans, 45

adrenaline, 36, 60, 119

agenda, 80, 88

aggression, 7, 10, 11, 12, 13, 15, 16, 17, 19, 20, 33, 35, 38, 39, 40, 53, 58, 59, 63, 64, 65, 67, 74, 75, 77, 85, 87, 89, 97, 98, 102, 107, 118, 120, 122

aggressive, 9, 11, 12, 15, 18, 19, 22, 26, 27, 29, 49, 58, 59, 63, 66, 69, 70, 72, 74, 75, 77, 78, 80, 82, 85, 87, 88, 89, 90, 91, 95, 99, 105, 106, 108, 109, 118

aggressive situations, 9, 15, 49, 63

aggressor, 7, 12, 17, 18, 19, 21, 22, 23, 24, 33, 39, 40, 43, 49, 51, 52, 54, 55, 57, 59, 64, 65, 66, 68, 69, 71, 77, 89, 90, 95, 97, 98, 99, 100, 102, 103, 104, 108, 111, 112, 113, 114, 115, 116, 121, 122

alternatives, 48

anger, 10, 27, 37, 51, 52, 58, 60, 63, 79, 81, 101, 104, 105, 106, 107, 109, 110

Anger, 7, 57, 124

angry, 16, 19, 21, 23, 27, 28, 37, 41, 51, 52, 54, 59, 79, 90, 94, 99, 101, 104, 105, 106, 121

appointment time, 40

argumentative, 39

armed, 26

Assault, 33

assertive, 26, 29

assertiveness, 29

Assessing situations, 66

assessments, 45, 67, 68, 93

attacking, 52

awareness, 7, 61, 77, 91

back up, 69, 71

bar, 17, 38

basic human needs, 17, 78

battery, 33, 34

be prepared, 49, 73

black and white, 81, 104

blades, 106, 107

blaming, 81

body language, 16, 18, 20, 21, 55

boundaries: Setting, 84, 86, 108

Bullying, 7, 117, 118

calm, 18, 20, 21, 22, 23, 50, 51, 52, 53, 57, 58, 61, 64, 70, 71, 89, 98, 100, 102, 103, 104, 107

127

calmer environment, 77

care, 9, 10, 11, 12, 22, 32, 44, 47, 63, 67, 70, 72, 74, 75, 82, 84, 85, 90, 94, 98, 102, 106, 117, 120, 121

childcare, 43, 74, 85, 100, 110

children, 32, 43, 85, 100, 101, 102, 104, 108, 110

choice, 67, 86, 93, 109

choices, 43, 85, 104, 105, 106, 107, 108

class room, 65

client, 44, 66, 67, 70, 72, 73, 78, 82, 83, 91, 94, 95, 121

club, 38

colleagues, 71, 78, 81, 82, 90

communicating, 36

communication, 18, 39, 40, 59

complacent, 92

complain, 23, 24, 80, 89

confident, 27, 71, 73, 112

conflict resolution, 7, 15, 16, 17, 19

consequences, 66

control, 24, 25, 44, 50, 58, 64, 65, 80, 84, 85, 87, 101, 109, 111

crime, 49

crowd control, 35

cultures, 36

customer, 23, 24, 25, 26, 38, 75, 78, 90

customer safety, 38

customer's, 25, 26, 38, 75

customers, 24, 25, 80, 95

danger, 31, 63

de-escalation, 11, 39

disruptive, 103

dissolve the anger, 105

Distraction, 98

Doctor, 41, 121

emotional, 7, 19, 21, 27, 28, 63, 77, 81

employee, 9, 13

employers, 9, 10

environment, 38, 77, 91, 95

escape route, 69, 91

escapes routes, 116

evidence, 44, 92, 93

exercise, 79

Exercise, 55, 74, 94

Exits, 94

eye contact, 37

fatal, 114

feelings, 26, 29, 59, 60

fight, 19, 36, 42, 52, 57, 59, 60, 66, 106, 108

fights, 70

fixed focus of attention, 58

focus their attention, 117

Forward Planning, 93

frustrated, 97

gang, 26, 70, 119

group beliefs, 120

gun, 112, 113

head-butting, 114

Health and Safety at Work Act 1974, 9

help, 19, 22, 25, 33, 35, 41, 50, 55, 60, 61, 66, 80, 83, 85, 97, 98, 99, 106, 108, 110, 111, 121

Hindsight, 93

history, 44, 45, 68, 70, 92

hit you, 54

hospital, 40, 73, 91, 98, 102, 118

hospitals, 70, 79, 84, 120

instinctive, 10

interruption, 99

intimidating, 36, 63

Keep distance, 54

kicking, 111, 114

knife, 90, 106, 111, 114, 115

knives, 26, 67

lethal weapon, 90

life threatening, 11, 111, 116

listen, 80, 99, 100

listening, 22, 40, 51, 55, 101

maintain your safety, 47, 114

maintaining safety, 16, 66

make better decisions, 48, 64

manage the situation, 13, 50, 64, 66, 71, 82, 120

manager, 48, 49, 51, 67, 68

managing aggression, 7, 11, 20, 97

Managing incidents, 64

meetings, 12, 69, 82, 122

needs, 7, 10, 48, 77, 81, 82, 93, 119, 121

Negligence, 32

negligent, 9, 26, 32, 33, 71

Negotiating, 108

Non-physical, 7, 97

non-threatening, 20, 21, 52, 55, 99, 107

noradrenalin, 60

nursing, 10, 12, 67

offence, 28

Offering good choices, 42

Offering support, 97

office, 42, 48, 72, 91, 94

options, 42, 43, 85, 106, 115

paranoid, 94

patient, 38, 41, 46, 47, 92, 121

patient and their needs, 41

personal space, 7, 35, 36, 37

physical pain, 79

physically, 45, 52, 59, 66, 71, 103

physically aggressive, 52

plan, 25, 45, 66, 67, 69, 71, 74, 80, 93, 110, 111

Planned ignoring, 99, 100, 101

planning, 42, 51, 69, 80, 95, 105

points of view, 59, 99

police, 25, 26, 33, 49, 66, 69, 71

Police, 35

primitive response, 57

problems, 45, 78, 93

public transport, 84

punching, 111

purpose, 80

racism, 118

Rapport, 17, 18

Reasonable Force, 31

129

recording, 2, 13, 121

reduce the chances of an attack, 55

reduce the risk, 93

relaxed, 20, 21, 61, 64, 79, 94

reporting, 13, 121

Reporting of Injuries, Diseases and Dangerous Occurrences Regulations 1995 (RIDDOR), 9

resident, 70, 75

residential care homes, 120

restraint, 11, 88

retail, 11, 28, 75

risk, 9, 10, 25, 26, 39, 44, 45, 50, 67, 68, 70, 74, 90, 91, 93, 95, 107, 113

risk assessment, 68

risks, 7, 25, 35, 44, 49, 67, 68, 74, 91, 92, 93, 95, 113

Routines, 110

sanction, 85, 109

scared, 59

scenario, 29

serious, 31, 49, 114

serious incidents, 49

sharp, 90

shifts, 94, 111, 117

shop, 26, 37, 42, 43, 49, 69, 91, 98, 102, 106

shoplifter, 42, 43, 48, 49, 50

shoplifters, 42

shoplifting, 42, 69, 105, 106

situations, 5, 12, 13, 16, 23, 24, 27, 37, 39, 42, 47, 49, 50, 56, 67, 69, 70, 73, 74, 75, 77, 78, 82, 83, 84, 85, 90, 91, 93, 94, 95, 102, 109, 111, 112, 116, 121, 122

skills, 10, 11, 12, 16, 39, 97, 122

social worker, 46, 93

staff, 9, 10, 12, 13, 15, 24, 25, 28, 38, 42, 43, 44, 45, 46, 47, 48, 56, 64, 67, 68, 69, 70, 71, 72, 73, 77, 78, 82, 84, 85, 86, 87, 94, 95, 102, 107, 108, 109, 110, 111, 117, 118, 120, 121, 122; training, 5, 9, 10, 11, 12, 15, 16, 32; turnover, 10

Staff changeovers, 94

Staff meetings, 122

state of mind, 27, 28, 29, 58, 104, 107

stealing, 42

stranger, 36

strategies, 7, 12, 16, 17, 56, 59, 67, 97, 101, 113

stress hormones, 60

support, 5, 11, 97, 98, 119, 121

supportive, 5, 55

surprise, 57

survival response, 59

swearing, 101

sympathetic, 55

teaching, 12, 67

team, 38, 56, 73, 95, 108, 116, 120, 121, 122

technique, 27, 99, 104

techniques, 10, 11, 12, 15, 16, 17, 39, 97, 122

teenager, 44

therapist, 83

Thinking, 39

threat, 19, 27, 47, 57, 58, 63, 64, 69, 80, 107

tolerance, 37, 77, 78, 79

train conductor, 48

understanding, 15, 18, 98, 122

upset, 28

victim, 19, 65

violence, 7, 9, 10, 11, 12, 13, 15, 16, 17, 20, 33, 35, 38, 40, 44, 63, 64, 67, 68, 70, 74, 75, 77, 87, 92, 118, 120, 122

violent, 9, 15, 18, 21, 70, 71, 72, 74, 75, 82, 106

vulnerable, 46, 114

waiting room, 37, 78

weapons, 68, 111, 112, 114

winding people up, 39

witnesses, 72

workplace, 11, 12, 38, 56, 70, 74, 90, 116, 118, 122

young people, 47, 90, 100, 101, 102, 104, 108

young person, 45, 47, 63, 90, 101, 106

Printed in the United States
210081BV00004B/154/P